Published by Creative Education
P.O. Box 227, Mankato, Minnesota 56002
Creative Education is an imprint of The Creative Company

Design and production by Blue Design
Printed in the United States of America

Photographs by Getty Images (Brian Bahr, Al Bello, Doug Benc, Steve Green/MLB Photos, Otto Greule Jr/Stringer, John Grieshop/MLB Photos, Scott Halleran/Allsport, Jed Jacobsohn, Paul Jasienski, Mitchell Layton, Mitchell Layton/MLB Photos, Doug Pensinger, Rich Pilling/MLB Photos, Eliot J. Schechter, Ezra Shaw, Don Smith, Jamie Squire, Mary Steinbacher, Matthew Stockman)

Library of Congress Cataloging-in-Publication Data

Peterson, Sheryl.
The story of the Florida Marlins / by Sheryl Peterson.
p. cm. — (Baseball: the great American game)
Includes index.
ISBN-13: 978-1-58341-488-0
1. Florida Marlins (Baseball team)—History—
Juvenile literature. I. Title. II. Series.

GV875.F56P48 2007
796.357'6409759381—dc22   2006027460

First Edition
9 8 7 6 5 4 3 2 1

Cover: Pitcher Dontrelle Willis
Page 1: Shortstop Edgar Renteria
Page 3: Pitcher Josh Johnson

THE STORY OF THE
FLORIDA MARLINS

by Sheryl Peterson

JOSH BECKETT

Florida Marlins

Game 6 of the 2003 World Series was scoreless in the fifth inning. New York Yankees pitcher Andy Pettitte had been stifling them, but the Florida Marlins finally scored a run when second baseman Luis Castillo swatted the ball into Pro Player Stadium's right field for a single, allowing shortstop Alex Gonzalez to race home from second base. Then, outfielder Juan Encarnacion lofted a sacrifice fly high into right field, and outfielder Jeff Conine tagged from third and slid across home plate in a dusty cloud to notch Florida's second run. The two runs were more than enough. Masterful Marlins hurler Josh Beckett pitched a complete-game, 2–0 shutout, and the improbable Marlins, playing David to New York's Goliath,

became World Series champs. Marlins fans went wild as Yankees fans stood in stunned silence. Strong pitching and clutch hitting had prevailed, giving the 11-year-old Marlins their second world championship.

MIAMI'S NEW FISH

o most people, the mention of Miami, Florida, conjures up images of palm trees, sandy beaches, and tourists. Blessed with mild climates year-round and unrivaled ocean access, America's southernmost resort city is a popular recreation destination. Miami, whose population is half Hispanic, is a city diverse in people, food, language, and music.

Miami caters to action-oriented visitors from around the globe with some of the world's top sports venues. Since the early part of the 20th century, baseball has also been a staple in South Florida, which has long provided warm spring training sites for several major-league clubs from northern locations. Miami also saw many colorfully named pro teams of other baseball leagues come and go, such as the Miami Magicians, Miami Wahoos, and Miami Beach Flamingos.

When the National League (NL) was permitted by Major League Baseball to expand in 1993, a baseball franchise was awarded to South Florida, with Wayne Huizenga, owner of the Blockbuster Video corporation and the Miami Dolphins football team, as the new team's owner. No longer would baseball head north every late spring. Huizenga, an avid deep-sea fisherman, named the team. "I chose Marlins," he said, "because the fish is a fierce fighting adversary that tests your mettle." The team's uniforms and the outfit of its lively

MARLINS

[6]

mascot, Billy the Marlin, continued the ocean theme in hues of teal and silver.

Miami's Joe Robbie Stadium was converted from a football facility to a dual-use arena that could accommodate baseball. As attractive as the palm tree-landscaped venue was, however, fans soon learned that the open-air stadium became very hot during summer days and was frequently plagued by thunderstorms at night. "Pick up the park and move it 500 miles north," quipped sportswriter Jeff Merron, "and you've got a real winner." Regardless of the weather, Florida fans fell in love with the team, snapping up season tickets before the club ever took the field.

A TEAL MONSTER AND MORE

The Marlins' ballpark was originally called Joe Robbie Stadium, then Pro Player Stadium, and today is known as Dolphin Stadium. It is often compared with Fenway Park in Boston, as both stadiums have notoriously tall left-field walls, with hazardous nooks and crannies in the outfield fence that create tough bounces for outfielders. Florida's wall is nicknamed "The Teal Monster" as a nod to Fenway's famous "Green Monster." Other quirks abound in the park. A clock atop the center-field wall sometimes robs hitters of home runs. A notch in deep center field creates a mysterious area known as the "Bermuda Triangle," where players can hit the ball 433 feet without it ever leaving the park, leading to frequent triples. Because of Miami's summer heat, which often "cools off" to about 85 degrees on August nights, Dolphin Stadium is not always a ballpark fans want to visit. The stadium does, however, get top ratings from visitors for its hot dogs and also offers hearty local fare, such as Cuban sandwiches and conch fritters. In the seventh-inning stretch, while the cheerleading Marlin Mermaids dance on one dugout, mascot Billy the Marlin, the friendly fish with the killer snout, boogies on the other.

The Marlins' first player acquisitions included hustling catcher Benito Santiago, pitcher Bryan Harvey, and hard-hitting outfielder Jeff Conine. On April 5, 1993, a sold-out crowd of 42,334 spectators packed the stands of the modified Joe Robbie Stadium. The Marlins won their first official game, 6–3, over the Los Angeles Dodgers, but the rest of the expansion team's season had as many low points as the "Python" roller coaster at Florida's Busch Gardens Amusement Park.

Still, dedicated fans in southern Florida found several heroes to cheer for during that opening 64–98 season. Santiago made history by slamming the Marlins' first home run, but the players who made the most early noise were Conine and fellow outfielder Gary Sheffield. The brawny Conine, acquired in an expansion draft from the Kansas City Royals' minor-league system, hit .292 and drove in 79 runs in his inaugural year in Florida.

Sheffield, a Florida native who arrived in 1993 via a midseason trade from the San Diego Padres, led the Marlins' offense in 1994 by slamming 27 home runs in just 87 games. With Conine and Sheffield in charge, the "Fighting Fish" posted a 51–64 record during the strike-shortened 1994 season. Conine and Sheffield weren't the only bright spots, though. Hard-throwing hurler Robb Nen demonstrated his future All-Star form by saving 15 games, while fleet young center fielder Chuck Carr swiped 32 bases. Marlins manager Rene Lachemann saw these performances as reason for optimism. "I like the direction we are headed," he told reporters.

PITCHER · DONTRELLE WILLIS

Dontrelle Willis, nicknamed "D-Train," was a minor-leaguer with the Chicago Cubs when he was traded to the Marlins in 2002. At first, Willis, capable of throwing heat approaching 100 miles per hour, attempted to smooth out his herky-jerky delivery style, but then realized that his unusual method aided in his deception of batters. The enthusiasm and broad smile Willis frequently exhibited on the field endeared him to Marlins fans, as did his uncommonly good batting ability. In June 2006, he collected his 50th career win, moving him past A.J. Burnett on the Marlins' all-time victory list.

DONTRELLE WILLIS
PITCHER

FLORIDA
MARLINS

STATS

Marlins seasons: 2003–present

Height: 6-4

Weight: 200

- **2003 NL Rookie of the Year**

- **2-time All-Star**

- **First Marlins pitcher to win 20 games in a season (2005)**

- **3.44 career ERA**

Gary Sheffield's powerful forearms generated great bat speed, resulting in jaw-dropping home runs.

GARY SHEFFIELD

An All-Star in three different decades, Benito Santiago suited up for nine major-league teams in his career.

BENITO SANTIAGO

CATCHER · CHARLES JOHNSON

Florida native Charles "Chuck" Johnson was born and raised in Fort Pierce and attended the University of Miami. He was a starting catcher on the U.S. baseball team in the 1992 Barcelona Olympics and then joined the Marlins via the first round of the 1994 amateur draft. Johnson got a key base hit during the pivotal Game 7 of the 1997 World Series to bring home outfielder Moises Alou and tie the game. Johnson left Florida in 1998 but returned three seasons later. During the 2001 season, he donated $100 to charity for every opposing base stealer he threw out.

STATS

Marlins seasons: 1994–98, 2001–02

Height: 6-3

Weight: 225

- **2-time All-Star**
- **4-time Gold Glove winner**
- **167 career HR**
- **570 career RBI**

CHARLES JOHNSON
CATCHER

FLORIDA
MARLINS

MARLINS DIVE DEEP

Due to the lingering players' strike, the 1995 season got off to a late start, but once it did, the Marlins faithful saw even greater fireworks. Fans were awed by a run of 14 straight home wins at Joe Robbie Stadium in July. Catcher Charles Johnson, a former All-American at the nearby University of Miami, put on a defensive clinic behind the plate, his quick hands and cannon arm stopping many would-be base stealers dead in their tracks. And with 35-year-old third baseman Terry Pendleton wielding a sure glove at the "hot corner" and adding 11 years of experience to the clubhouse, the young Marlins ended their third year with a respectable 67–76 record.

Prior to the 1996 season, the Marlins signed hurlers Kevin Brown and Al Leiter. The left-handed Leiter wasted no time in winning over Florida fans, striking out six batters as he fired the franchise's first no-hitter in an 11–0 whitewashing of the Colorado Rockies on May 11. By mid-July 1996, with the Marlins mired in a slump and eight games under .500, Huizenga fired manager Rene Lachemann and moved vice president John Boles onto the bench in an effort to spark the team. The move seemed to help, and the Marlins finished the season with an 80–82 mark to place third in the NL Eastern Division.

EDGAR RENTERIA

EDGAR RENTERIA – Just 20 years old during his 1996 rookie season, Renteria quickly became a standout shortstop. He found the spotlight a year later by driving home the championship-clinching run in Game 7 of the 1997 World Series.

FIRST SPLASH

The front-page headlines shouted "Play Ball" and "Batter Up," words Florida sports fans had been longing to hear for years. The Florida Marlins made their major-league debut on April 5, 1993, against the Los Angeles Dodgers, a team that was founded in 1890. Under sunny Florida skies, a festive atmosphere pervaded Joe Robbie Stadium, including the world-renowned Florida A&M marching band and tributes to the men responsible for giving baseball a summer home in the fourth-largest state in the country. Hall of Fame outfielder Joe DiMaggio, then age 78, tossed out the ceremonial first pitch. Then, 45-year-old Charlie Hough, who grew up near Miami, took the mound for the expansion Marlins, and a crowd of 42,334 fans stood and cheered his first pitch. "I'll never forget it," said Hough. "All those years I watched baseball come in the spring and then leave." The crowd roared again when Hough struck out the first two batters with his famous knuckleballs in a 1-2-3 first inning. Hough pitched solidly until reliever Bryan Harvey eventually took over for the save in the 6–3 Florida win. At the final out, in a scene more befitting an October playoff game than an opening day contest, leaping, shouting Marlins players ran onto the field to celebrate the historic victory.

JOE ROBBIE STADIUM

JEFF CONINE

MARLINS

Jeff Conine was the only player to appear on Florida's 1993 roster and its 1997 and 2003 World Series teams.

FIRST BASEMAN · DERREK LEE

Derrek Lee got his baseball ability naturally, being the son of Leon Lee and the nephew of Leron Lee, both of whom played for the Lotte Orions baseball team of Kowasaki, Japan. Lee was the total package of power, speed, and defensive ability. He was a giant at first base, standing 6-foot-5, yet he showed impressive range and was surprisingly nimble and quick around the bag. Lee learned his baseball work ethic as a boy growing up in Japan with his father, where he came to respect the game in such small ways as to refrain from spitting on the playing field.

DERREK LEE
FIRST BASEMAN

FLORIDA MARLINS

STATS

Marlins seasons: 1998–2003

Height: 6-5

Weight: 205

• **2-time Gold Glove winner**

• **2005 All-Star**

• **2005 NL leader in BA (.335)**

• **216 career HR**

Boles returned to the Marlins' front office in 1997, and former Pittsburgh Pirates skipper Jim Leyland was hired as the third Florida manager. Adding experience to the club's already talented lineup were burly third baseman Bobby Bonilla, pitcher Alex Fernandez, and outfielder Moises Alou. The additions spelled instant success, as Bonilla, Alou, Johnson, Conine, and Sheffield all hit at least 17 homers on the year, and Fernandez, Brown, and Leiter won 17, 16, and 11 games, respectively. Blazing to a 92–70 season finish, the young Marlins finished just behind the Atlanta Braves in the NL East race and captured the NL Wild Card berth into the playoffs.

In their first postseason, the Marlins met the San Francisco Giants in a first-round matchup. Incredibly, the underdog Marlins proved themselves the more unflappable team in the showdown, getting clutch hits from Alou and shortstop Edgar Renteria to win Games 1 and 2. In Game 3, Devon White, a center fielder famed for his great speed, slugged a sixth-inning grand slam to propel Florida to a 6–2 victory and wrap up a three-game sweep of the Giants. "This is great," said White, "but we have another hill to climb."

The NL Championship Series (NLCS) pitted the Marlins against their division rivals, the Braves. Stepping up to the challenge, Brown gave stellar pitching performances in Games 1 and 6, and Cuban-born, rookie pitcher

SECOND BASEMAN · LUIS CASTILLO

Castillo's trademark was the "slap and dash" game, as he often worked deep pitch counts and then showed off wicked foot speed after making contact. An excellent bunter, he frequently ranked among the league leaders in infield hits, and even though he was a natural right-handed hitter, he could bat left as well. Castillo put together a 35-game hitting streak in 2002, the longest ever by a second baseman. On the defensive side, Castillo was a dynamo in the field and boasted one of the strongest arms of any second-sacker in the game. "Louie" spent off-seasons in his native Dominican Republic.

STATS

Marlins seasons: 1996–2005

Height: 5-11

Weight: 190

• 3-time Gold Glove winner

• 3-time All-Star

• 2-time NL leader in stolen bases

• .293 career BA

LUIS CASTILLO
SECOND BASEMAN

FLORIDA MARLINS

Livan Hernandez earned the series Most Valuable Player (MVP) award by winning two games in dominant style. The Marlins toppled the Braves in six games, claiming a berth in the World Series.

The Marlins faced the Cleveland Indians in the 1997 "Fall Classic," and in front of a rowdy crowd in Miami's newly renamed Pro Player Stadium, they captured Game 1 by a 7–4 score thanks largely to a three-run homer by Alou. The two teams battled to a split over the first six games, forcing a deciding Game 7 in Florida. In the bottom of the ninth inning, with Florida down 2–1, Marlins second baseman Craig Counsell smacked a sacrifice fly to score Alou from third and force extra innings. After a scoreless 10th, the Marlins found themselves with the bases loaded and two outs in the 11th. In dramatic fashion, Renteria hammered a ground ball up the middle that brought Counsell home, and the party was on.

In one breathtaking moment, the young Marlins became the fastest expansion team ever to win a World Series. "What an amazing season," exclaimed Leyland. "For these guys to be the first team to ever win as a Wild Card just shows what heart they have."

Well-traveled third baseman Bobby Bonilla spent just one season in Florida but earned a World Series ring.

BOBBY BONILLA

PRESTON WILSON

Preston Wilson showed off his blossoming home run power in 1999 before thin crowds at Pro Player Stadium.

FIRE-SALE FRENZY

Incredibly, by opening day of the 1998 season, most of the players responsible for the Marlins' 1997 world championship were gone. Despite the fact that the team had drawn more than 500,000 fans during the 1997 postseason, Huizenga sold off most of his highest-paid players, claiming he could not meet the large payroll. Florida fans watched in disbelief as Nen, Brown, White, and Conine were replaced by inexpensive minor-league prospects.

Once the 1998 season started, even more key players, such as Bonilla and Johnson, were let go. Sheffield was shipped off to the Dodgers for star catcher Mike Piazza . . . who was then promptly dealt to the New York Mets. Florida fans felt betrayed, and the team crashed and burned, falling to a lowly 54–108 finish less than a year after standing atop the baseball world.

With new ownership in 1999 (Huizenga sold the team to local businessman John Henry), and the return of Boles as manager, the team rallied with new hope. A group of youngsters—including outfielders Preston Wilson and Cliff Floyd, second baseman Luis Castillo, first baseman Derrek Lee, and shortstop Alex Gonzalez—began to show its stuff during the 64–98 season. The Marlins were still in the NL East basement, but Wilson warned, "The rest of the league better get ready. Our time is coming soon."

At the start of the new century, the Marlins' fortunes rode on a promising new pitching staff, as rookie starters Brad Penny and A.J. Burnett, as well as closer Antonio Alfonseca, were all counted on to boost the Marlins up the NL East standings. The team's starting pitchers struggled, but thanks to stellar play by Castillo (.334 batting average and a major-league-leading 62 stolen bases), Wilson (31 homers and 121 runs batted in, or RBI), Lee (28 homers), and Alfonseca (a major-league-leading 45 saves), the 2000 Marlins surged to a third-place finish in the division.

Florida's 79–82 record in 2000 was impressive, considering the injuries that plagued the team. Gonzalez suffered a strained knee, Castillo endured back problems, and outfielder Cliff Floyd played courageously throughout the season with a painful wrist injury. Floyd's gutsy play in particular was an inspiration to the team. "Going out there every day and killing your-

WILD-CARD LUCK

In 1995, Major League Baseball introduced a new playoff system that included the use of a Wild Card team in each league. This meant that, for the first time, two teams each year would make the playoffs without winning their division. The new format was not without controversy. Some fans and experts thought the Wild Card weakened baseball by allowing teams with relatively poor records into the postseason, while others countered that the Wild Card would create exciting playoff games and give a greater number of fans hope during the season. The Florida Marlins "lucked out" by gaining the Wild Card entry both seasons they won the World Series. In 1997, the Marlins won the Wild Card with a 92–70 record and went on to take out the Giants, Braves, and Indians for the title, becoming the first Wild Card team to win it all. In 2003, the Marlins clinched the Wild Card spot with a 91–71 record, and once again, they capitalized on it for a world title. "A Wild Card team has to play hard throughout the season," said Marlins outfielder Jeff Conine in defense of the playoff format. "Wild Card players are hungrier and better prepared going into the postseason."

At 6-foot-4 and 260 pounds, sinkerball pitcher Brad Penny was among the game's biggest hurlers.

BRAD PENNY

THIRD BASEMAN · MIKE LOWELL

Lowell was a master of the old hidden ball trick, in which an infielder mimes throwing the ball to the pitcher and then hides the ball before tagging out the fooled base runner when he takes a lead. Lowell's career was plagued by injury and illness—including cancer—but he always fought his way back onto the field. Although he often cracked jokes about his slow foot speed, Lowell was a smart runner who made the most of his scoring chances. In 1999, the third baseman won the Tony Conigliaro Award, given to a player who has overcome a major obstacle and continued to succeed.

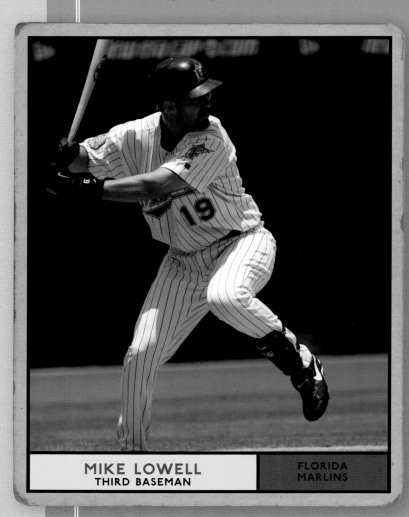

MIKE LOWELL
THIRD BASEMAN

FLORIDA MARLINS

STATS

Marlins seasons: 1999–2005

Height: 6-3

Weight: 210

- **3-time All-Star**

- **2005 Gold Glove winner**

- **.273 career BA**

- **163 career HR**

self for the team . . . ," said third baseman Mike Lowell. "Cliff showed us a champion's heart."

Before the 2001 season, in an effort to inject some old magic into the young team, Florida added World Series hero Charles Johnson back onto the roster, putting a sure glove behind the plate and a reliable bat in the lineup. Another key addition arrived in the middle of the season, when former Cincinnati Reds great Tony Perez replaced John Boles as the club's manager.

In 2001, the Marlins' young pitchers showed improvement, and the club played well early in the season before fading to finish fourth in the division with a 76–86 record. Off the field, talk of contraction—or the elimination of struggling franchises—began to swirl, and the young Marlins were identified as a possible candidate for termination. Adding to the unrest, team owner John Henry left to buy the Boston Red Sox, leaving the Marlins high and dry.

THE COLDEST GAME

The National Weather Service had warned World Series fans. A mass of cold air pushing down from Canada was headed for Cleveland and Game 4 of the 1997 World Series. The Cleveland Indians' Jacob's Field, situated close to Lake Erie, was likely to receive lake-effect snow. The first two games of the series had been played in sunny, 80-degree Florida, but on October 22, Marlins fans exchanged their T-shirts and sandals for earmuffs and fur-lined boots. Hot coffee became the chilly evening's fastest-selling concession beverage. It was a tough night for both batters and pitchers, and players on both sides wore long underwear, turtlenecks, and gloves on their throwing hands. Several bats broke like brittle toothpicks amid the flurries, fielders and base runners had trouble keeping their footing, and batters got more of a sting when they connected with a fastball. The evening's low temperatures (38 degrees, and only 18 with the wind chill) made the game the coldest ever in World Series history. As the game ended in a 10–3 defeat for Florida, Marlins president Don Smiley said, "I love hunting ducks in October, and today was the Super Bowl of duck-hunting weather."

CLIFF FLOYD

In 2001, his best and final full Marlins season, Cliff Floyd batted .317 with 31 home runs and 103 RBI.

SHORTSTOP · ALEX GONZALEZ

Born in Venezuela, Gonzalez broke into the big leagues in 1998 with the Marlins. Blessed with great agility and fielding range, he was valued more for his defense than his offense. Gonzalez played a key role in the 2003 World Series win against the Yankees. After going 1 for 13 in the postseason, he hit a majestic, walk-off home run in the 12th inning of Game 4 to give the Marlins a 4–3 victory and a two-games-to-two series tie. As that dramatic shot proved, Gonzalez was deceptively strong at the plate, and he had enough speed to frequently turn singles into doubles.

STATS

Marlins seasons: 1998–2005

Height: 6-0

Weight: 200

- **1999 All-Star**
- **425 career RBI**
- **90 career HR**
- **17-game hitting streak (2005)**

ALEX GONZALEZ
SHORTSTOP

FLORIDA
MARLINS

Jeffrey Loria, an art dealer and former managing partner of the Montreal Expos, finally stepped in and bought the Florida club.

Even though Castillo produced a team-record 35-game hitting streak, Pro Player Stadium resembled a ghost town through much of the 2002 season. Signs of doom remained, despite an ultimately respectable 79–83 record, as the popular Floyd was traded away during the team's fifth straight losing season. After the season, Wilson was dealt away for outfielder Juan Pierre, All-Star catcher Ivan "Pudge" Rodriguez was added, and the Marlins embarked on a new direction that emphasized pitching and speed in hopes of becoming competitive once again. "I think the 2003 season is going to be the year of the Marlins," said Rodriguez.

HOOK, LINE, AND CLINCHER

hrough the first weeks of the 2003 season, the Marlins floundered in last place as ace pitcher A.J. Burnett was sidelined with an elbow injury. Fortunately, a young pitching powerhouse named Dontrelle "D-Train" Willis arrived on the scene and quickly became a sensation. Fans packed Pro Player Stadium to marvel at the 6-foot-4 Willis's old-school, high-kicking windup and blazing fastballs. Jeff Conine also returned, to the delight of dedicated "Mr. Marlin"

LEFT FIELDER · CLIFF FLOYD

Cliff Floyd was a natural athlete. A star from the day he picked up a baseball bat, he was also a gifted football and basketball player in high school. The tall and powerful outfielder read pitchers well and had enough speed to frequently take an extra base. Although injured during the Marlins' 1997 World Series win, Floyd was the first one out of the dugout to celebrate when shortstop Edgar Renteria ended Game 7 with an 11th-inning single. When healthy and manning left field, Floyd used his long arms and loping stride to snag many balls that initially seemed uncatchable.

CLIFF FLOYD
LEFT FIELDER

FLORIDA
MARLINS

STATS

Marlins seasons: 1997–2002

Height: 6-4

Weight: 230

- **2001 All-Star**

- **2-time Marlins team MVP**

- **781 career RBI**

- **213 career HR**

DONTRELLE WILLIS

An unusual windup, side-armed throwing style, and assortment of quality pitches made Dontrelle Willis a star.

CENTER FIELDER · PRESTON WILSON

Preston Wilson was both smart and talented. Valedictorian of his Miami high school class, he broke into the big leagues with the New York Mets at age 23. He soon demonstrated superior arm strength and throwing accuracy from center field and showed that he could catch up with even the speediest fastball at the plate. Wilson wielded a big bat, was able to rip hits to all parts of the field, and had enough speed to post 3 seasons of 20-plus stolen bases. The center fielder came by his talent naturally, as he was the nephew of former New York Mets outfielder Mookie Wilson.

PRESTON WILSON
CENTER FIELDER

FLORIDA
MARLINS

STATS

Marlins seasons: 1999–2002

Height: 6-2

Weight: 193

- **2003 All-Star**

- **.264 career BA**

- **1992 *Baseball America*'s High School Player of the Year**

- **2003 NL leader in RBI (141)**

fans. The infusion of new blood continued with the hiring of a surprising new manager: tough-talking, 72-year-old Jack McKeon. "Age is just a number to me," said McKeon, the oldest manager in the game. "I feel about 35."

The 2003 Marlins crept up the NL East ladder as McKeon challenged his team. "I know it's a tall order," he said, "but I believe in miracles." Florida fans came to believe too, as the team climbed from a 19–29 start all the way to a 91–71 finish. On September 26, 2003, the club clinched the NL Wild Card in a stirring 4–3 win over the Mets, with pitcher Carl Pavano collecting the win and Ugueth "Oogie" Urbina recording the save. In doing so, the Marlins became just the ninth team in major-league history to come from 10 or more games under .500 during a season to make the playoffs.

On October 4, the Marlins defeated the San Francisco Giants 7–6 in Game 4 of the NL Division Series (NLDS), winning the series three games to one. The game ended with a flourish, as a throw to home by outfielder Jeff Conine with two outs in the ninth inning led to a home-plate collision between Marlins catcher Ivan Rodriguez and Giants first baseman J.T. Snow; the play marked the first time in major-league history that a playoff series ended with the tying run being thrown out at home plate. The "Fighting Fish" continued to fly high as they then beat the Chicago Cubs in Games 1, 5, and 6 of the NLCS. Rising young pitcher Josh Beckett took the mound for Game 7 and topped the Cubs in a 9–6 comeback victory at Chicago's Wrigley Field to seal the pennant. Against all

A.J. BURNETT

THE UGLY INNING

For five scoreless innings at Atlanta's Turner Field on September 22, 2002, Marlins star hurler A.J. Burnett, just off the disabled list with a right elbow bruise, surrendered only two hits to the Braves. But one inning later, when Burnett turned the mound over to right-handed reliever Julian Tavarez, the bizarre ensued. With one out, Braves first baseman Julio Franco scored from second on a single by third baseman Chipper Jones, even though replays showed that Marlins outfielder Juan Encarnacion's throw to the plate was in time to tag out Franco. Then Marlins third baseman Mike Lowell fielded a bouncer close to third base and turned to tag Braves outfielder Gary Sheffield. Lowell trapped Sheffield between third and short, but then decided to throw to second to try for a double play. Jones beat the throw, Sheffield advanced, and Lowell, who was hoping to force Jones out at second and then tag Sheffield in a rundown, was charged with an error. To cap the unsightly inning, Tavarez was then ejected after he plunked Braves catcher Henry Blanco with a pitch. "All the screws came loose . . .," said Lowell after the Marlins lost the game 4–1. "It's an inning we'd all rather rewind, but we can't."

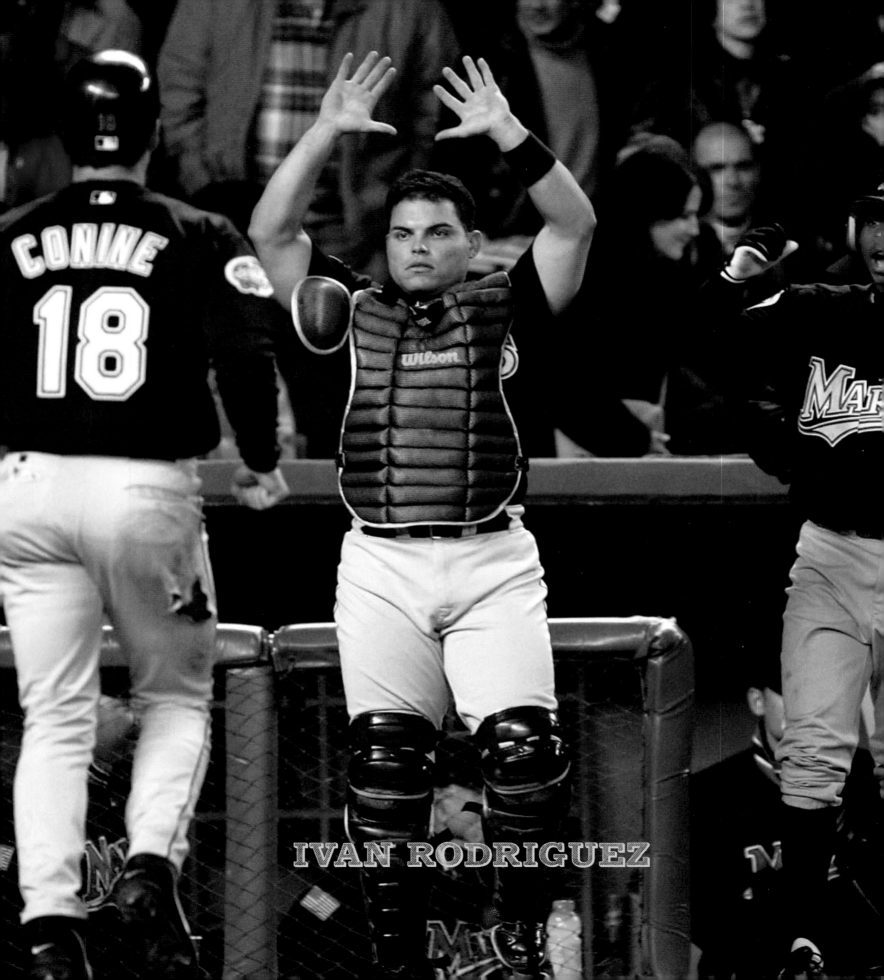

IVAN RODRIGUEZ

odds, the Marlins were back in the World Series.

The 2003 World Series, Major League Baseball's 100th, was an intriguing matchup; the legendary New York Yankees versus the underdog, 11-year-old Marlins. The Florida team entered Yankee Stadium and, behind a solid pitching effort by Penny, stole Game 1 by a 3–2 score. The Yankees won the next two games, but in Game 4 in Miami, Florida shortstop Alex Gonzalez, who was batting a horrific .094 in the playoffs, homered deep to left field in the 12th inning to win the game and even the series. In Game 5, Penny allowed just two Yankees runs over seven innings to give Florida a 6–4 win. The Marlins were just one win away.

Florida began Game 6 with confidence and with Beckett—pitching on only three days' rest—on the hill. Beckett, a superstitious pitcher who took pains never to touch the white line on his way to the pitcher's mound and back, was irked by the media's constant reminders of the Yankees' unmatched championship tradition. "All I knew," said Beckett before the game, "was that we were going to get World Series rings on opening day next season."

With Beckett and Yankees left-hander Andy Pettitte locked in a classic pitchers' duel, something had to give. And something did: Luis Castillo's 0-for-14 batting slump. "Baseball is highs and lows," the second baseman later explained. "I was pretty low, but every game, every at bat is another chance." Unable to manage much off of Pettitte, the Marlins finally scratched out a run in the fifth inning when Castillo slapped a Pettitte offering to right field. Yankees outfielder

JOSH BECKETT

Karim Garcia charged and made a strong throw home, but Gonzalez—running hard from second base—made a crafty slide, wiggling away from catcher Jorge Posada's swipe tag and brushing his left hand across the plate to give the Marlins a 1–0 lead. Florida added a second run an inning later.

Beckett held off the Yankees through eight innings and then worked a swift ninth, ending the game by scooping up a chopped grounder down the first-base line and tagging out Posada. As Rodriguez flung his facemask skyward in celebration of his preseason prediction-turned-reality, Beckett became the first pitcher since Minnesota Twins hurler Jack Morris in 1991 to toss a complete-game shutout in a deciding World Series game. The young Florida Marlins, with a 2–0 win over the Yankees, had just completed one of the biggest upsets in World Series history.

RIGHT FIELDER · GARY SHEFFIELD

Gary Sheffield made history when he was voted onto the 1993 NL All-Star team, as he became the first player from a first-year expansion team to start in a "Midseason Classic." Sheffield rewrote the Marlins' record books in 1996, his fourth season with the club, blasting 42 home runs, batting .314, and scoring 118 runs—all despite being walked 142 times. "The Sheff" slammed three big hits in Game 3 while leading the Marlins to their 1997 World Series win. He was among the game's most recognizable batters, due largely to his dramatic bat waggle while awaiting pitches.

GARY SHEFFIELD
RIGHT FIELDER

FLORIDA MARLINS

STATS

Marlins seasons: 1993–98

Height: 6-0

Weight: 215

- **.297 career BA**

- **455 career HR**

- **1992 Major League Player of the Year**

- **9-time All-Star**

FLORIDA FIGHTS ON

T he following year, the Marlins went 83–79 to post their third winning season, but there would be no World Series repeat, as they finished nine games behind the Houston Astros in the race for the 2004 NL Wild Card. The preseason departure of Rodriguez hurt the team, and a series of rain-outs due to hurricanes in Florida factored in the Marlins' late-season downfall.

The 2005 Marlins seemed poised to return to the playoffs as late as September 13, but then lost 12 of their next 14 games and closed the season with a final record of 83–79. After the last game, Jack McKeon announced his retirement and was replaced by former Yankees bench coach Joe Girardi.

When the Marlins decided to part ways with World Series heroes Burnett, Gonzalez, and Castillo before the 2006 season, it seemed Florida was in rebuilding mode again. Things looked even bleaker than expected when the Marlins started out a horrible 11–31. But the team then pulled together and roared back to a 78–84 finish, just missing the playoffs. Powering the offense was a terrific infield made up of slugging first baseman Mike Jacobs, All-Star second baseman Dan Uggla, speedy rookie shortstop Hanley Ramirez, and third baseman Miguel Cabrera, who batted a team-record .339 with 114 RBI.

JEFF CONINE

100TH ANNIVERSARY

The 2003 World Series marked the 100th anniversary of baseball's first modern Fall Classic. Appearing in the second World Series of their 11-year history were the plucky Florida Marlins. Opposite them, and making their sixth World Series appearance in eight years, were the daunting New York Yankees, who featured such stars as shortstop Derek Jeter and pitcher Roger Clemens. The young, inexpensive Marlins ($54-million payroll) went up against the veteran, high-priced Yankees ($164-million payroll) and toppled them four games to two to cap their remarkable Wild Card season. The anniversary series was, however, somewhat overshadowed by the NL

and American League (AL) Championship Series that postseason, when the Chicago Cubs and the Boston Red Sox—historically baseball's most hard-luck franchises—both went down in dramatic defeats. A Cubs fan interfered with Chicago left fielder Moises Alou's attempt to catch a foul ball in Game 6 of the NLCS, accidentally aiding the Marlins and helping to foil the Cubs, and Yankees third baseman Aaron Boone bopped an 11th-inning home run in Game 7 of the ALCS to break the hearts of Red Sox fans. The national media devoted extensive coverage to these events and the alleged "curses" that kept Chicago and Boston from the World Series.

MARLINS

But the team's greatest strength in 2006 was its new-look pitching staff, led by Willis and a collection of such talented rookies as Josh Johnson and Anibal Sanchez. Manager Fredi Gonzalez, who replaced Girardi after the season, hoped his young squad would keep rising in 2007. "We believe in each other, and that's all it takes," said Willis.

The history of the Florida Marlins is not a long one, but few teams can lay claim to so many highlights in so few seasons. With an all-time roster of baseball heroes that includes such names as Conine, Castillo, and Willis, and with two electrifying World Series wins in 1997 and 2003, cheers—and optimism— have rarely been in short supply in South Florida. And with today's Fighting Fish battling on, the thrills are likely to keep on coming.

MIKE JACOBS

Marlins fans hoped for big things from Mike Jacobs, an athletic first baseman with a picturesque swing.

MANAGER · JACK McKEON

Jack McKeon joined the Marlins in 2003 at age 72, making him the third-oldest manager in major-league history (behind Connie Mack and Casey Stengel). McKeon's age, however, did not temper his enthusiasm, and under his leadership, the Marlins improbably snagged a 2003 World Series win. McKeon earned the nickname "Trader Jack" in his early managerial days due to frequent player trades, and prior to managing, he played catcher for the Pittsburgh Pirates in the late 1940s. "I was the only player to hit three ways: left, right, and seldom," he once quipped. As the Marlins' skipper, McKeon often used such well-timed humor to motivate his team.

JACK McKEON
MANAGER

FLORIDA
MARLINS

STATS

Marlins seasons as manager: 2003–05

Height: 5-8

Weight: 198

Managerial Record: 1,011–940

World Series Championship: 2003

Alfonseca, Antonio 26

Alou, Moises 13, 20, 22

Beckett, Josh 5, 37, 41, 42

Billy the Marlin 7, 8

Boles, John 14, 20, 25, 29

Bonilla, Bobby 20, 25

Brown, Kevin 14, 20, 25

Burnett, A.J. 10, 26, 32, 39, 44

Cabrera, Miguel 44

Carr, Chuck 9

Castillo, Luis 5, 21, 25, 26, 32, 41, 44, 46

Conine, Jeff 5, 9, 20, 25, 26, 32, 37, 46

Counsell, Craig 22

Dolphin Stadium 8

Encarnacion, Juan 5, 39

Fernandez, Alex 20

first season 9, 16

Floyd, Cliff 25, 26, 29, 32, 33

Girardi, Joe 44, 46

Gold Glove award 13, 19, 21, 28

Gonzalez, Alex 5, 25, 26, 31, 41, 42, 44

Gonzalez, Fredi 46

Harvey, Brian 9, 16

Henry, John 25, 29

Hernandez, Livan 22

Hough, Charlie 16

Huizenga, Wayne 6, 14, 25

Jacobs, Mike 44

Joe Robbie Stadium 7, 8, 9, 14, 16

Johnson, Charles 13, 14, 20, 25, 29

Johnson, Josh 46

Lachemann, Rene 9, 14

Lee, Derrek 19, 25, 26

Leiter, Al 14, 20

Leyland, Jim 20, 22

Loria, Jeffrey 32

Lowell, Mike 28, 29, 39

major-league records 21

Marlins name 6

McKeon, Jack 37, 44

MVP award 22

NL batting championships 19

NL Championship Series 20, 37, 45

NL Division Series 20, 37

NL pennant 37

NL Wild Card 20, 26, 37, 45

Nen, Robb 9, 25

no-hitters 14

Pavano, Carl 37

Pendleton, Terry 14

Penny, Brad 26, 41

Perez, Tony 29

Piazza, Mike 25

Pierre, Juan 32

Pro Player Stadium 5, 8, 22, 32

Ramirez, Hanley 44

Renteria, Edgar 20, 22, 33

Rodriguez, Ivan "Pudge" 32, 37, 42, 44

Rookie of the Year award 10

Sanchez, Anibal 46

Santiago, Benito 9

Sheffield, Gary 9, 20, 25, 43

Smiley, Don 29

spring training 6

Tavarez, Julian 39

team records 44

Tony Conigliaro Award 28

Uggla, Dan 44

Urbina, Ugueth 37

White, Devon 20, 25

Willis, Dontrelle 10, 32, 46

Wilson, Preston 25, 26, 32, 36

world championships 5, 22, 26, 42, 43, 45, 46

World Series 5, 13, 22, 26, 29, 31, 33, 41, 42, 43, 45, 46